WILD CATS

Tigers

Anne Welsbacher
ABDO Publishing Company

visit us at
www.abdopub.com

Published by Abdo Publishing Company 4940 Viking Drive, Edina, Minnesota 55435.
Copyright © 2000 by Abdo Consulting Group, Inc. International copyrights reserved in all
countries. No part of this book may be reproduced in any form without written permission
from the publisher.

Printed in the United States.

Photo credits: Peter Arnold, Inc.

Edited by Lori Kinstad Pupeza
Contributing editor Morgan Hughes

Library of Congress Cataloging-in-Publication Data

Welsbacher, Anne, 1955-
    Tigers / Anne Welsbacher.
    p. cm. -- (Wild cats)
    Includes index.
    Summary: Describes the physical characteristics, social, feeding, and hunting
    behavior, and life cycle of the biggest of all wild cats.
    ISBN 1-57765-089-1
    1. Tigers--Juvenile literature. [1. Tigers.] I. Title. II. Series: Welsbacher, Anne,
    1955- Wild cats.
    QL737.C23W4523   2000
    599.756--dc21   98-13026
                                                        CIP
                                                        AC

Contents

Wild Cats around the World

*T*he tiger is one kind of wild cat. Many wild cats are big—sometimes bigger than people!

Tigers live in Siberia, India, and Asia. Long ago, tigers lived in other places, too. But many were killed by people. Today, some tigers are **extinct**.

Many wild cats have colors and marks that help them blend in with the land around them. Tigers do, too. They have stripes and face marks.

Tigers and other wild cats are good hunters. They have sharp claws and teeth. They use them to catch and eat animals.

Most cats do not like getting wet. But tigers love the water! They spend their days swimming!

Tigers have powerful jaws and sharp teeth.

Big Cat, Little Cat

Do you have a house cat? Your cat is like a wild cat in many ways. Big cats have sharp claws, just like house cats. And most cats can pull their claws into their paws.

Both wild cats and house cats have whiskers. They use them like fingers, to feel their way along small spaces.

Both big and little cats can see very well at night. Both lick themselves to keep clean. Both like to hunt.

Tigers, like most wild cats, like to be alone. Does your cat like to be around you? Or does it like to be alone?

House cats lie with their tails curled up close. But most big cats stretch their tails out long. Tigers, like house cats, can purr. They can also roar, like many wild cats!

Tigers need lots of room to live in. But they keep their babies, called cubs, hidden in small spaces. House cats keep their kittens in small, safe spaces, too.

Tigers use their whiskers to feel their way along small places.

A Closer Look

*T*igers are the biggest of all wild cats. The Siberian tiger is the biggest of all tigers. It can be 13 feet (4 meters) long! It can weigh as much as 845 pounds (383 kg).

The look of a tiger depends on where it lives. In cold climates, tigers are light yellow or almost white, to blend in with snow. They also are bigger. They have thicker coats and a lot of fat to keep them warm.

Tigers in warmer areas are smaller and have fur that is reddish or dark brown. They blend in with the shadows of a forest.

All tigers have dark stripes. Some have many stripes close together. Others have stripes with wider spaces between them. Every tiger has special stripes that are all its own, like your fingerprints!

Tigers have small ears with a patch of white on the back of each ear. They have very big paws, and very long claws. The tiger's claw is the length of your finger!

Tigers have long tails, sometimes almost as long as their bodies! They have four big teeth that look like fangs. These are called **canine** teeth.

Tigers that live in cold climates sometimes have white fur.

The Tiger at Home

The area and climate tigers live in is called their **habitat**. Tigers have many different habitats.

Some tigers live in jungles or evergreen forests. Others live on mountains, in swamplands, or on grasslands. Still others live in cold, snowy places.

Tigers like to live where they can find water to drink, food to eat, and lots of room to roam. They also need places where they can hide.

Tigers live in India, Asian countries, and Siberia. Tigers are named for the places they live.

The Chinese tiger lives in China. The Siberian tiger lives in Siberia. Siberia is very cold, so Siberian tigers are big and have thick coats.

Long ago, there were many more tigers in many countries. But most of them were hunted and killed. Today, tigers are **protected** in many places.

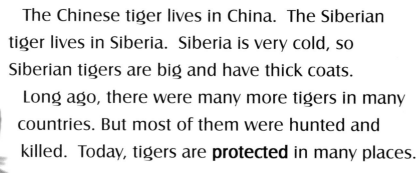

Siberian tigers in winter.

A Champion Swimmer

*T*igers love the water! Many tigers spend all day sitting in streams or rivers to keep cool!

Tigers are good swimmers. They have been known to swim three to four miles (five to seven km) at a time.

Tigers rest in the day when it is hot. They hunt in the evening when it is cool.

Tigers roar to keep other tigers and animals away. But sometimes, female tigers can be friendly. They purr and rub other tigers!

Tigers hunt by hearing because they have a poor sense of smell and poor eyesight.

Tigers eat 40 to 75 pounds (18 to 34 kg) or more of food. That would be like eating more than 100 apples! They take two or three days to eat every bit of food. Then they go without any food at all for another few days.

Tigers are great swimmers.

The Predator's Prey

*T*igers are **carnivores**. They also are called **predators**. Predators are animals that kill other animals for food. The animals they eat are called **prey**.

Tigers eat deer, antelopes, buffaloes, wild pigs, monkeys, porcupines, and birds. Sometimes they even eat small elephants or rhinoceroses! They also eat fish, crabs, frogs, and insects.

Tigers hunt about once a week. They hunt alone. They get close to their prey, about 60 feet (18 m) away. That's about the size of a large back yard.

Then, they spring forward with their strong back legs. They grab their prey and drag it to the ground.

They bite into the prey's neck with their long **canine** teeth. They break the animal's neck to kill it. Or they squeeze its throat until it cannot breathe.

When the animal is dead, the tiger drags it to a safe place. The tiger eats it over a few days. The tiger watches, snarls, and growls if others try to take its food away.

Two tigers feed on a sambar.

The Tiger's Territory

*T*igers like to be on their own. Male tigers do not like any other males near them. But male and female tigers get along.

Each male tiger has its own **territory**. In each territory there is one male tiger and one or more female tigers.

A tiger marks his territory with **urine**, by scratching the ground or a tree, or by rubbing his face on a tree. The smell the tiger leaves tells others that this territory belongs to him. Tigers know each other by their smells. Each smell is special.

Tigers need a lot of room, so each territory is big. Sometimes, one territory can be bigger than a small town! Even a small territory is as big as your whole neighborhood.

Tigers do not fight each other. They stay away from other tigers. They hunt and eat alone.

This tiger is marking its territory.

Cat Families

When a female tiger is three or four years old, she is ready to **mate** with a male tiger. After they mate, the female finds a **den**. After three to four months, the female gives birth to two or three cubs. They are about as big as your hand. She will keep her babies, called cubs, safely hidden in the den. The male tiger leaves.

The cubs are born with their eyes closed. They cannot walk. The newborn cubs **nurse** their mother.

Once or twice a week, the mother must leave the den to go hunting. The cubs are in danger. Other animals might eat them. She covers them with leaves to hide them. They stay very still.

The mother tiger brings her kill back to the nest to eat. They still drink milk from her. But when they are six weeks old, they begin to eat the meat she brings, too.

Three Sumatra cubs resting.

Growing Up

When they are about two weeks old, the cubs open their eyes. When they are 10 weeks old, they go with their mother on hunting trips.

They watch her hunt. They practice by pouncing on each other. They catch small birds.

When they are six months old, the cubs begin to hunt on their own. At this age, a tiger cub is as big as a large dog.

When they are around two years old, they are young adult tigers. They must leave to find their own **territories**.

Tigers that live in the wild could live about 15 years. Tigers that live in zoos or in parks where they are **protected** can live to about age 20.

Tigers live longer in zoos.

Glossary

Canines—long, fang-like teeth that help kill prey.

Carnivore—an animal that eats meat.

Den—a safe place made of rocks, bushes, or other things, where animals live and have babies.

Extinct—gone forever.

Habitat—the area and climate that an animal lives in.

Mate—to join in a pair in order to produce young.

Nurse—tiger cubs getting milk from their mother.

Predator—an animal that eats other animals.

Prey—an animal that is eaten by other animals.

Protected—animals that are protected cannot be hunted or hurt by people.

Territory—an area or place where an animal lives.

Urine—a yellowish watery liquid waste that mammals excrete.

Internet Sites

Tiger Information Center
http://www.5tigers.org/
The Tiger Information Center is dedicated to providing information to help preserve the remaining five subspecies of tigers. This is a great site, with many links, sound, and animation.

The Lion Research Center
http://www.lionresearch.org/
Everything you want to know about lions is here. Lion research and conservation in Africa, information on lion behavior, and updates from researchers in the Serengeti about specific lion prides.

The Cheetah Spot
http://ThingsWild.com/cheetah2.html
This is a cool spot with sound and animation. Lots of fun information.

Amur Leopard
http://www.scz.org/asian/amurl1.html
This site links you to some great zoo spots. Very informative.

These sites are subject to change. Go to your favorite
search engine and type in "cats" for more sites.

PASS IT ON

Tell Others What You Like About Animals!

To educate readers around the country, pass on interesting tips about animals, maybe a fun story about your animal or pet, and little-known facts about animals. We want to hear from you!

To get posted on the ABDO Publishing Company
Web site, email us at "animals@abdopub.com"
Visit us at www.abdopub.com

Index